Tapi Appreciates TEACHERS

Celebrating Every Lesson in Every Classroom

by MommyHooray

Teaching is the foundation of learning.
It shapes skills, habits, and confidence.
It prepares students for what comes next.

Tapi Appreciates Teachers
by MommyHooray

Written and published under the pen name MommyHooray.
Illustrations created using digital illustration tools.

Printed in the United States of America.

ISBN: 978-1-972071-23-6

For more stories and updates, visit:
https://sites.google.com/view/mommyhooray/

This book is dedicated to
the teachers who show up every day,
who guide, support, and care
in so many ways.
Because of you,
classrooms become places
where children feel safe to learn and grow.

With Googolplex Love,

MommyHooray

At school, teachers shine each day,
They guide and help us learn and play.
Let's meet them all with smiles so bright,
Ready to learn with all our might!

Classroom/Homeroom Teacher

You welcome us in with a warm hello,
You help us learn the things we need to know.
From songs we sing to stories we read,
You help us grow and meet each need.

What fun will we discover today?

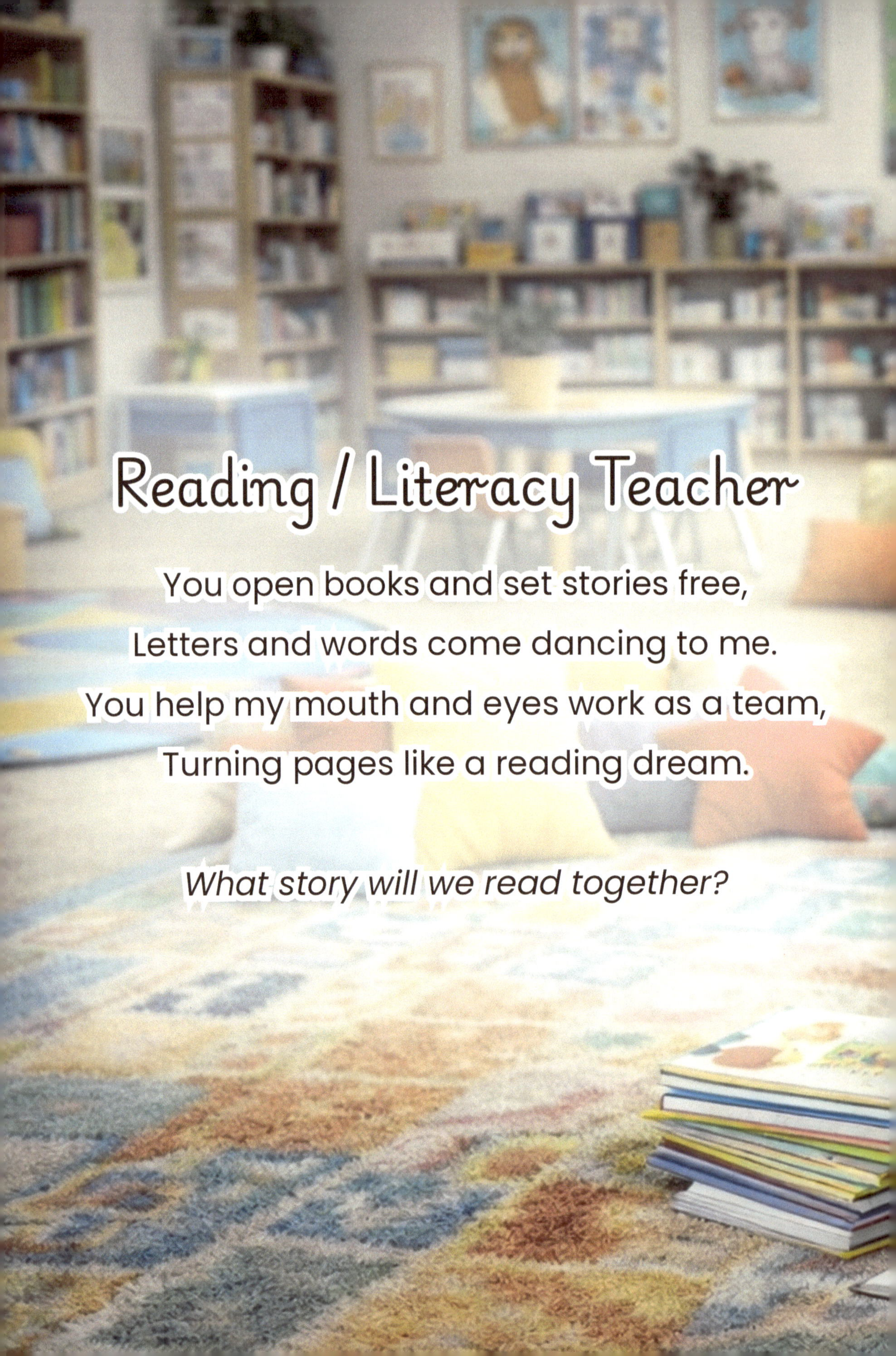

Reading / Literacy Teacher

You open books and set stories free,
Letters and words come dancing to me.
You help my mouth and eyes work as a team,
Turning pages like a reading dream.

What story will we read together?

Math Teacher

You bring out numbers big and small,
We count them up and stack them tall.
We sort and share and think it through,
Solving puzzles like we love to do.

Can we count something fun right now?

3

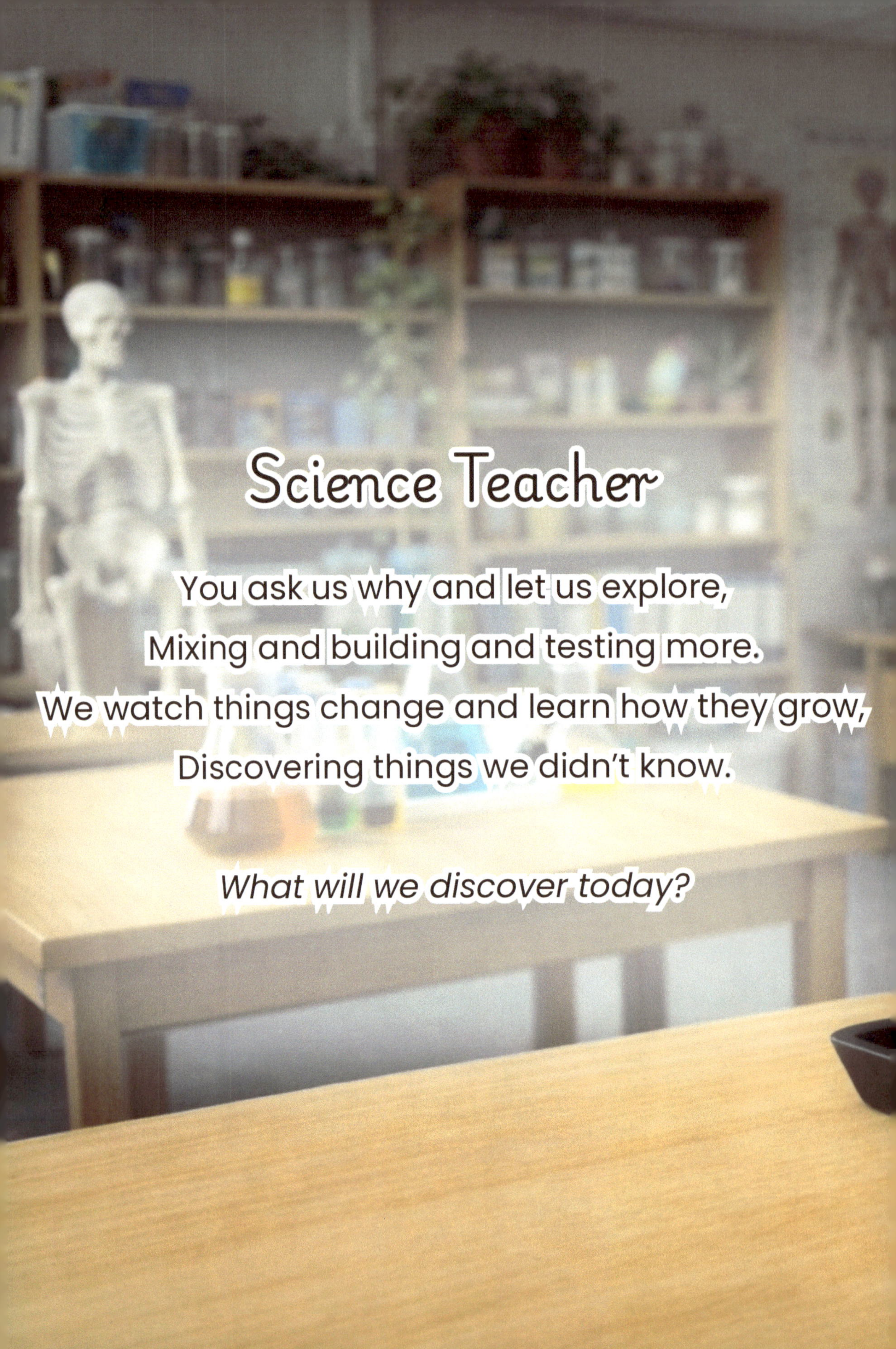

Science Teacher

You ask us why and let us explore,
Mixing and building and testing more.
We watch things change and learn how they grow,
Discovering things we didn't know.

What will we discover today?

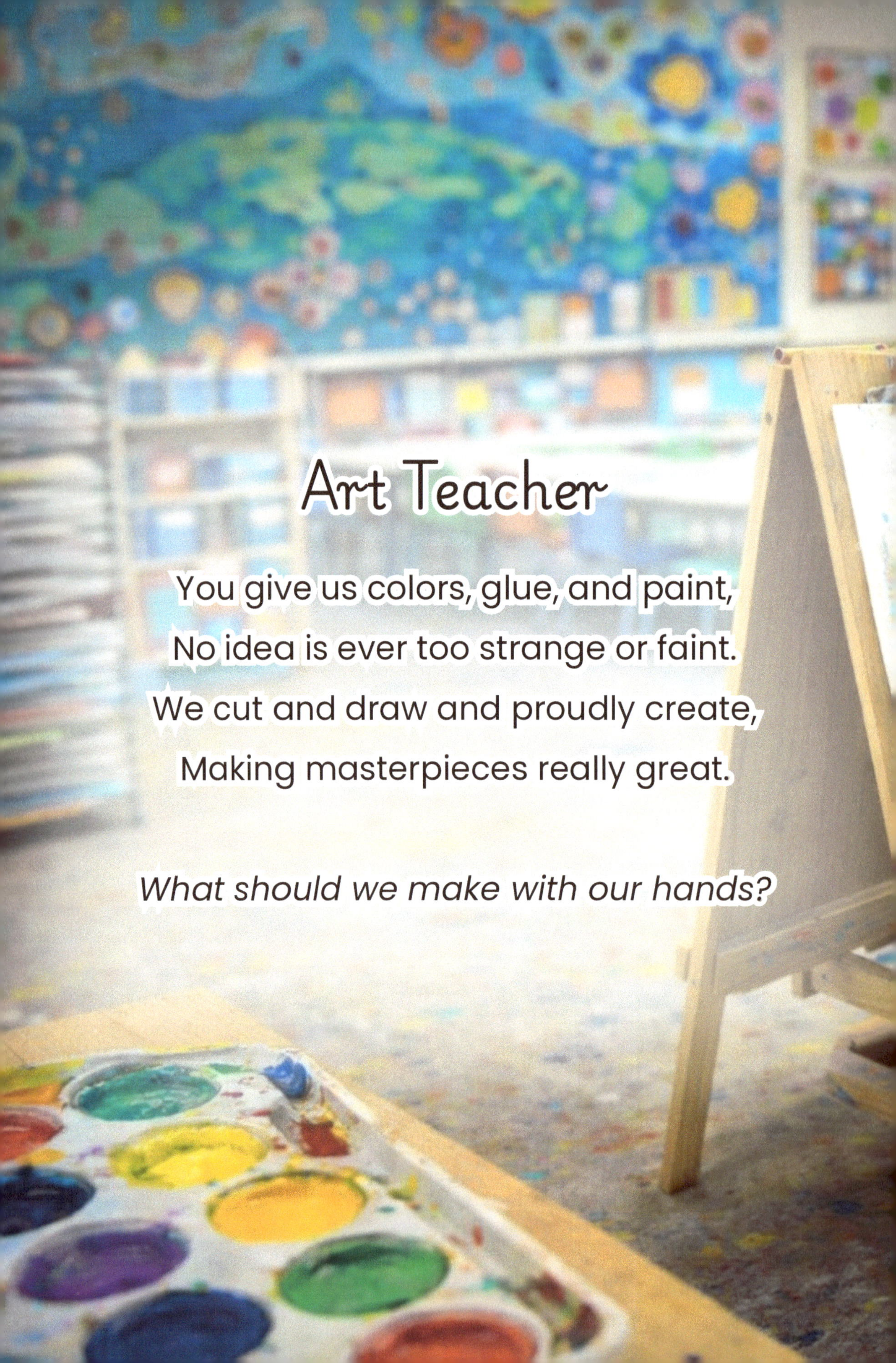

Art Teacher

You give us colors, glue, and paint,
No idea is ever too strange or faint.
We cut and draw and proudly create,
Making masterpieces really great.

What should we make with our hands?

Music Teacher

You start a beat and clap along,
Teaching us rhythm, sound, and song.
We tap our toes and sing out loud,
Making music feeling proud.

Shall we sing together now?

MUSIC

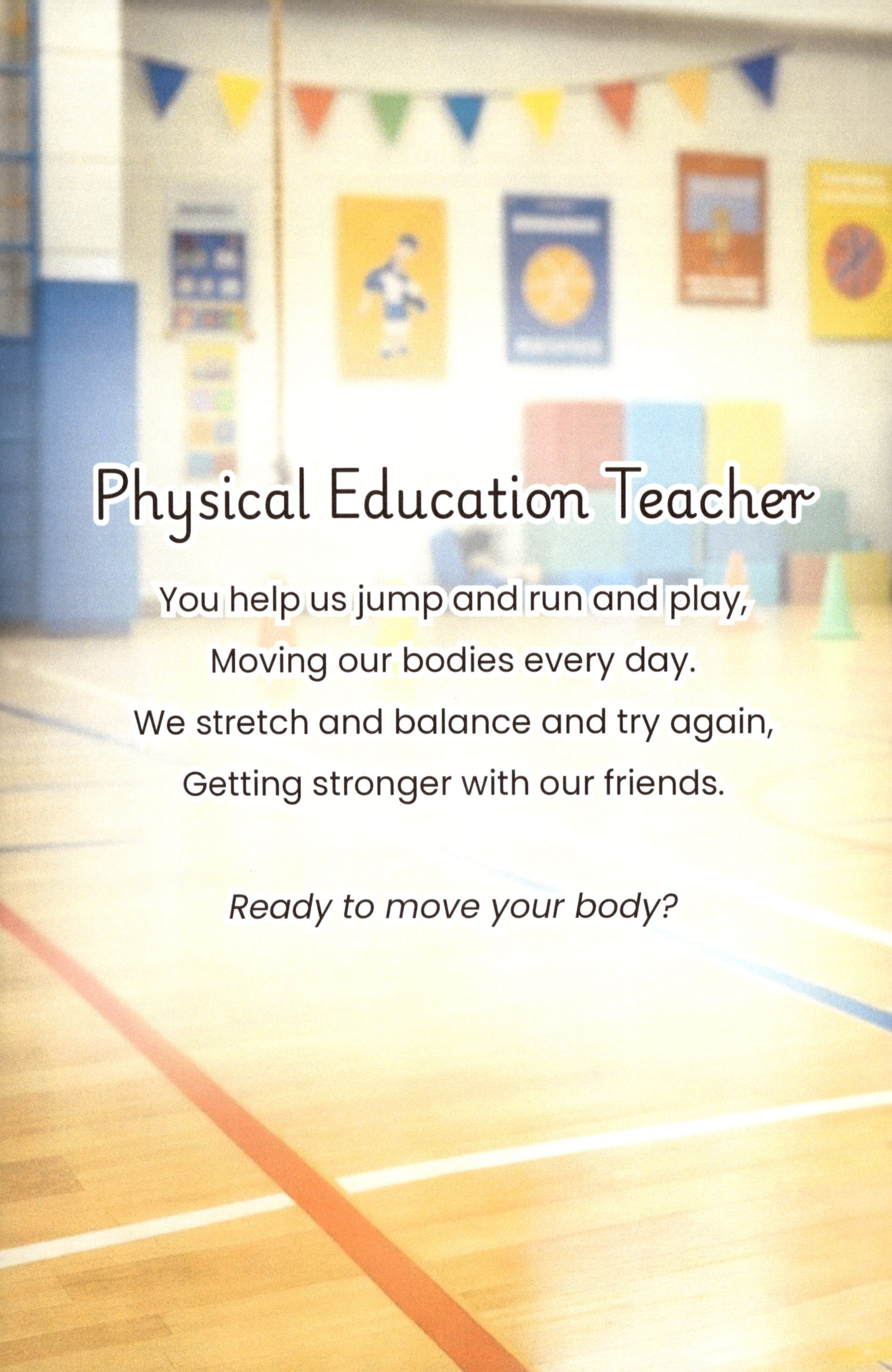

Physical Education Teacher

You help us jump and run and play,
Moving our bodies every day.
We stretch and balance and try again,
Getting stronger with our friends.

Ready to move your body?

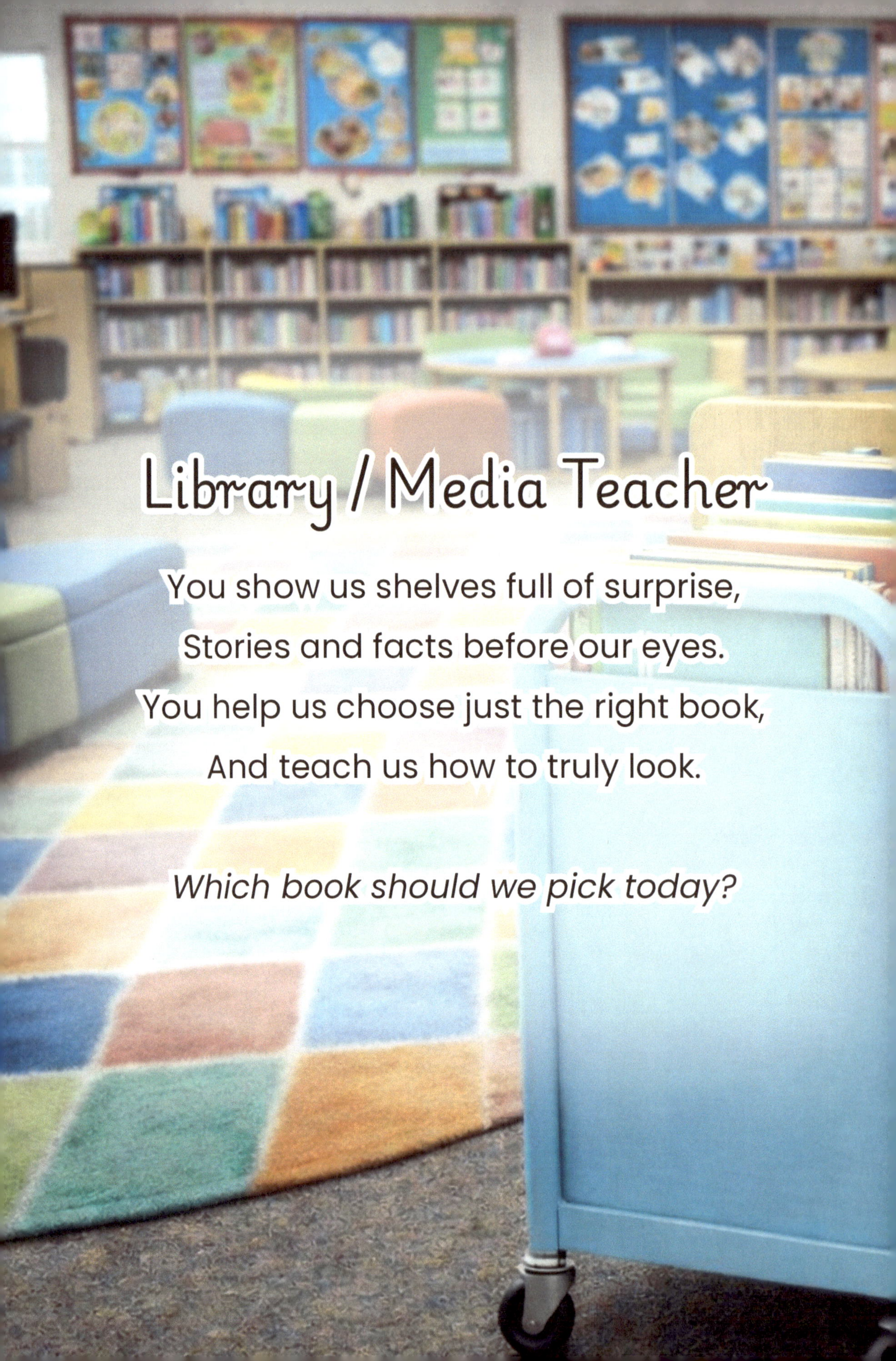

Library / Media Teacher

You show us shelves full of surprise,
Stories and facts before our eyes.
You help us choose just the right book,
And teach us how to truly look.

Which book should we pick today?

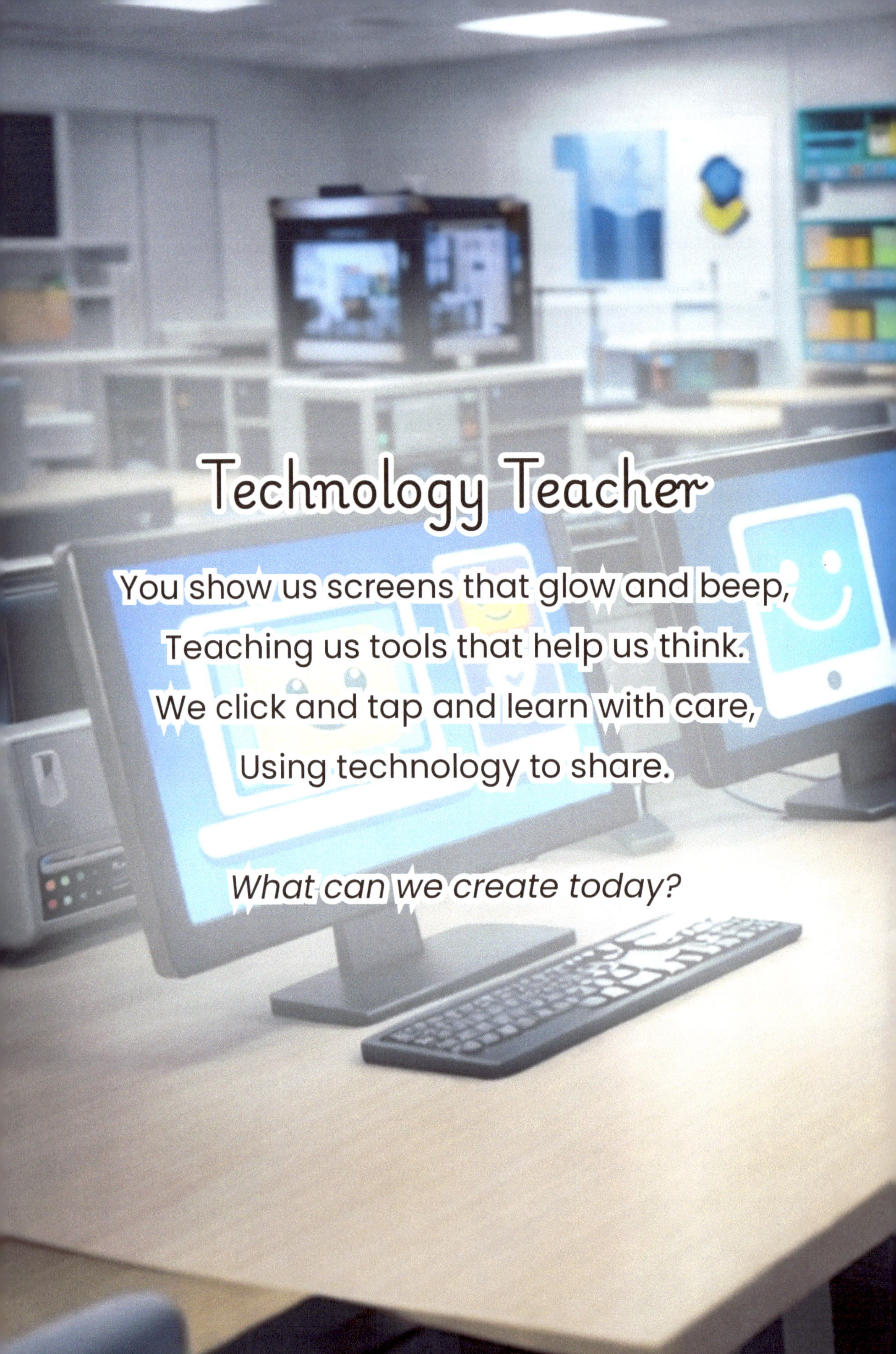

Technology Teacher

You show us screens that glow and beep,
Teaching us tools that help us think.
We click and tap and learn with care,
Using technology to share.

What can we create today?

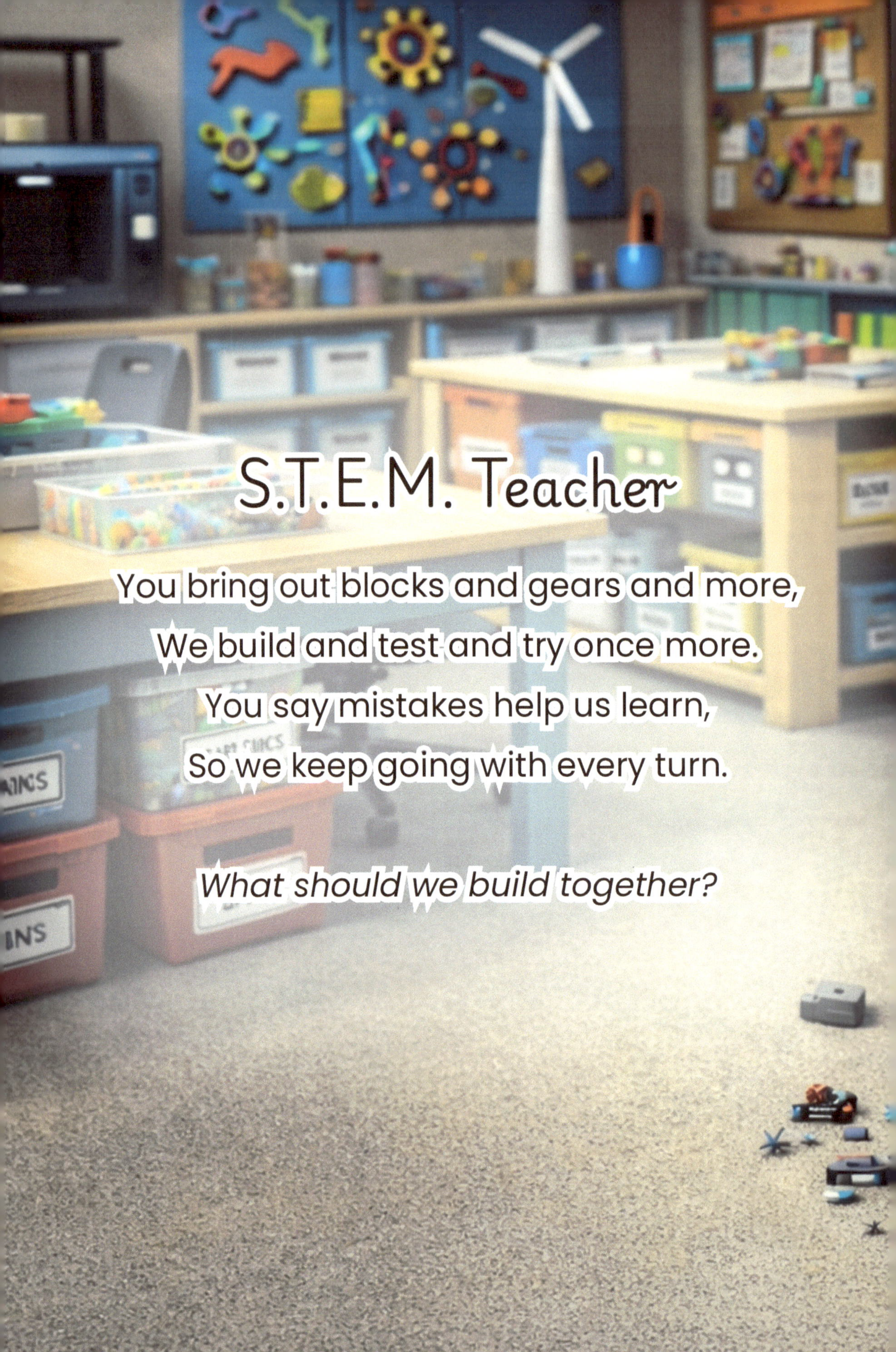

S.T.E.M. Teacher

You bring out blocks and gears and more,
We build and test and try once more.
You say mistakes help us learn,
So we keep going with every turn.

What should we build together?

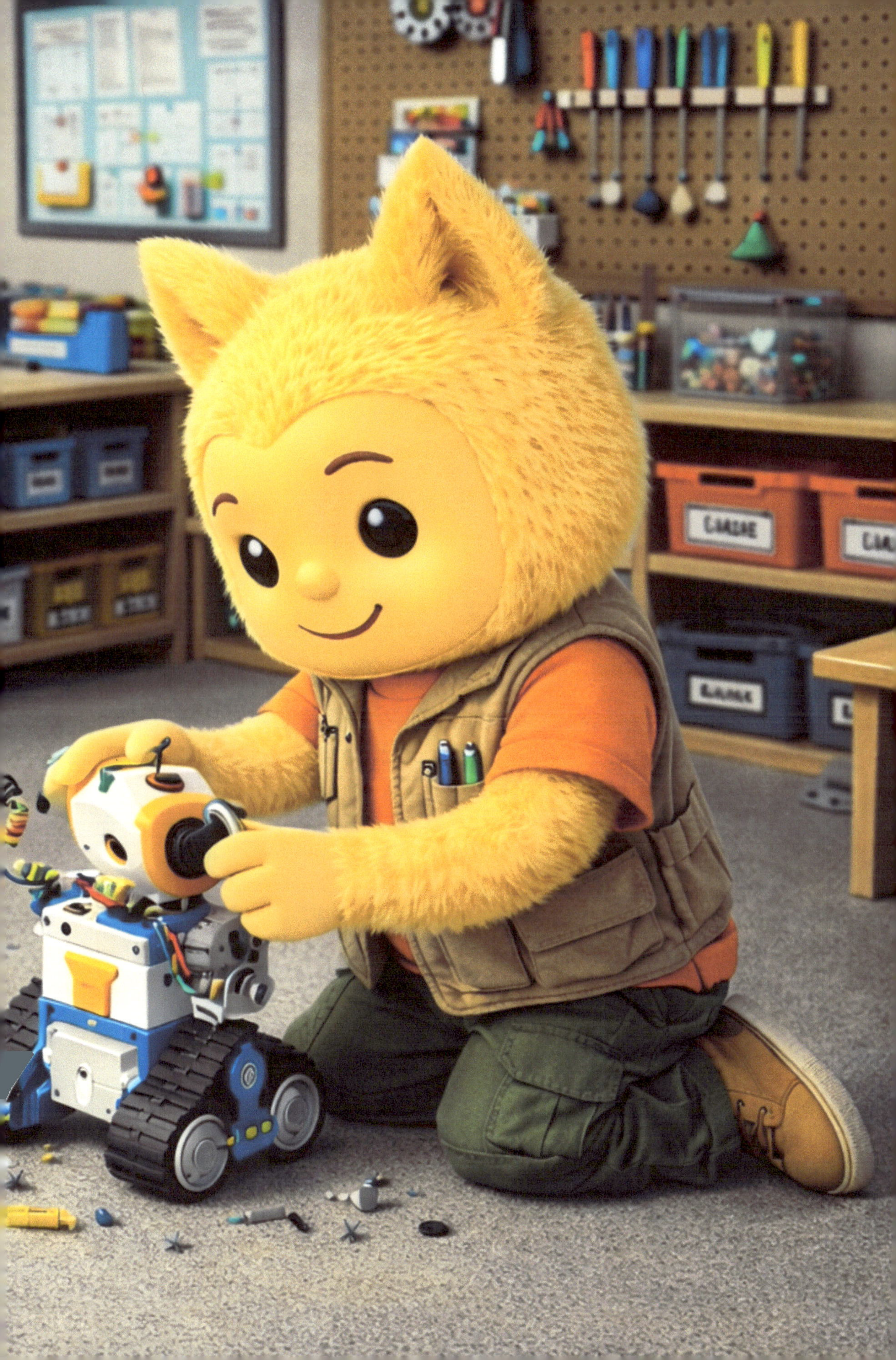

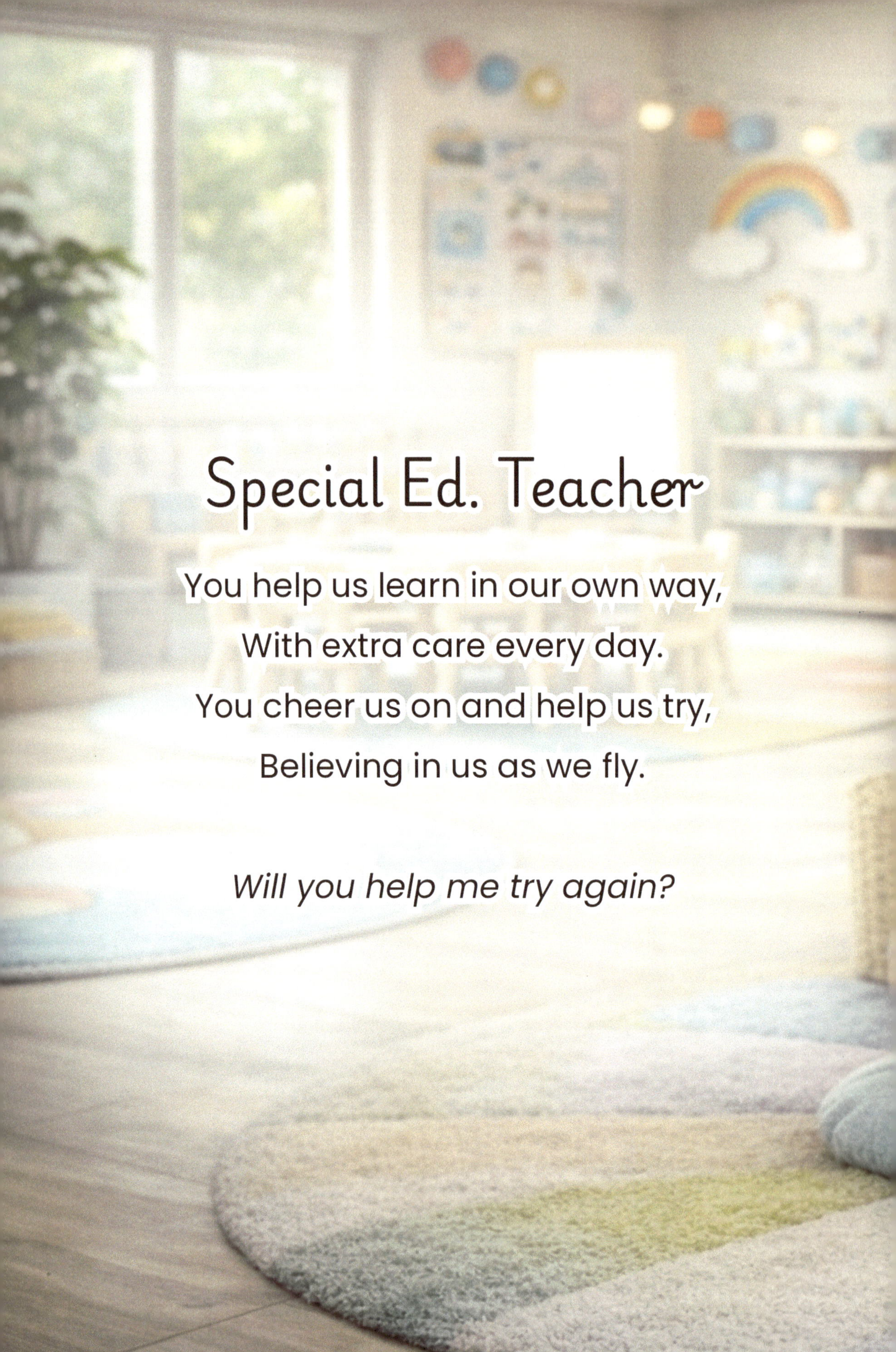

Special Ed. Teacher

You help us learn in our own way,
With extra care every day.
You cheer us on and help us try,
Believing in us as we fly.

Will you help me try again?

You teach new words from near and far,
Helping us say who we are.
We practice sounds and ways to speak,
Learning something new each week.

Can you teach me a new word?

Silla

Hello!
Hola!
book
libro
pencii
lápiz

School Counselor

You listen when I feel unsure,
Helping my heart feel safe and sure.
You help me name my big feelings too,
And find calm things I can do.

Can you help me feel better?

Speech & Language Pathologist

You help my words come out just right,
Practicing sounds with all my might.
We talk and listen and take our time,
Helping my voice learn how to shine.

Can we practice together?

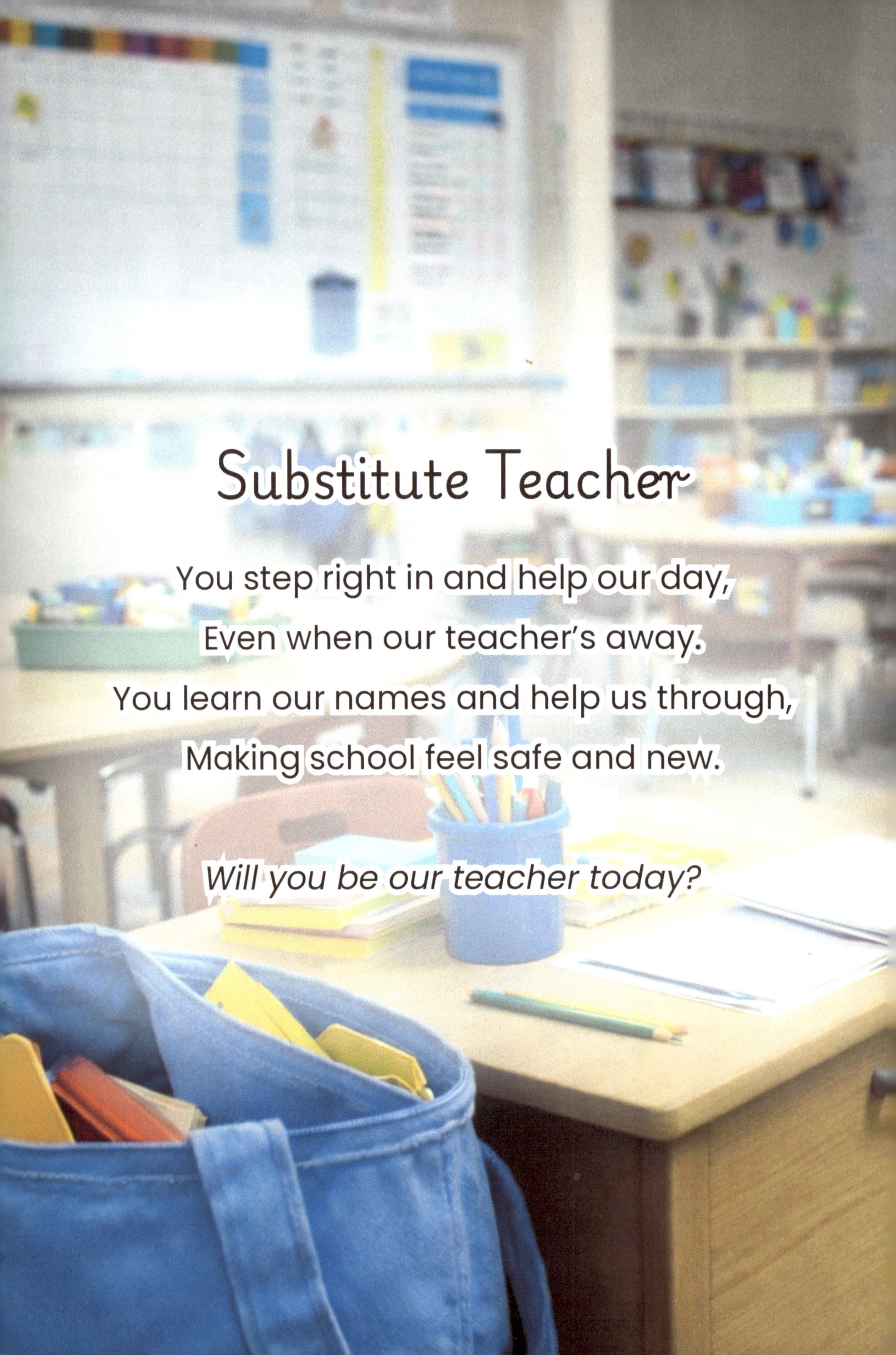

Substitute Teacher

You step right in and help our day,
Even when our teacher's away.
You learn our names and help us through,
Making school feel safe and new.

Will you be our teacher today?

Lesson Plan

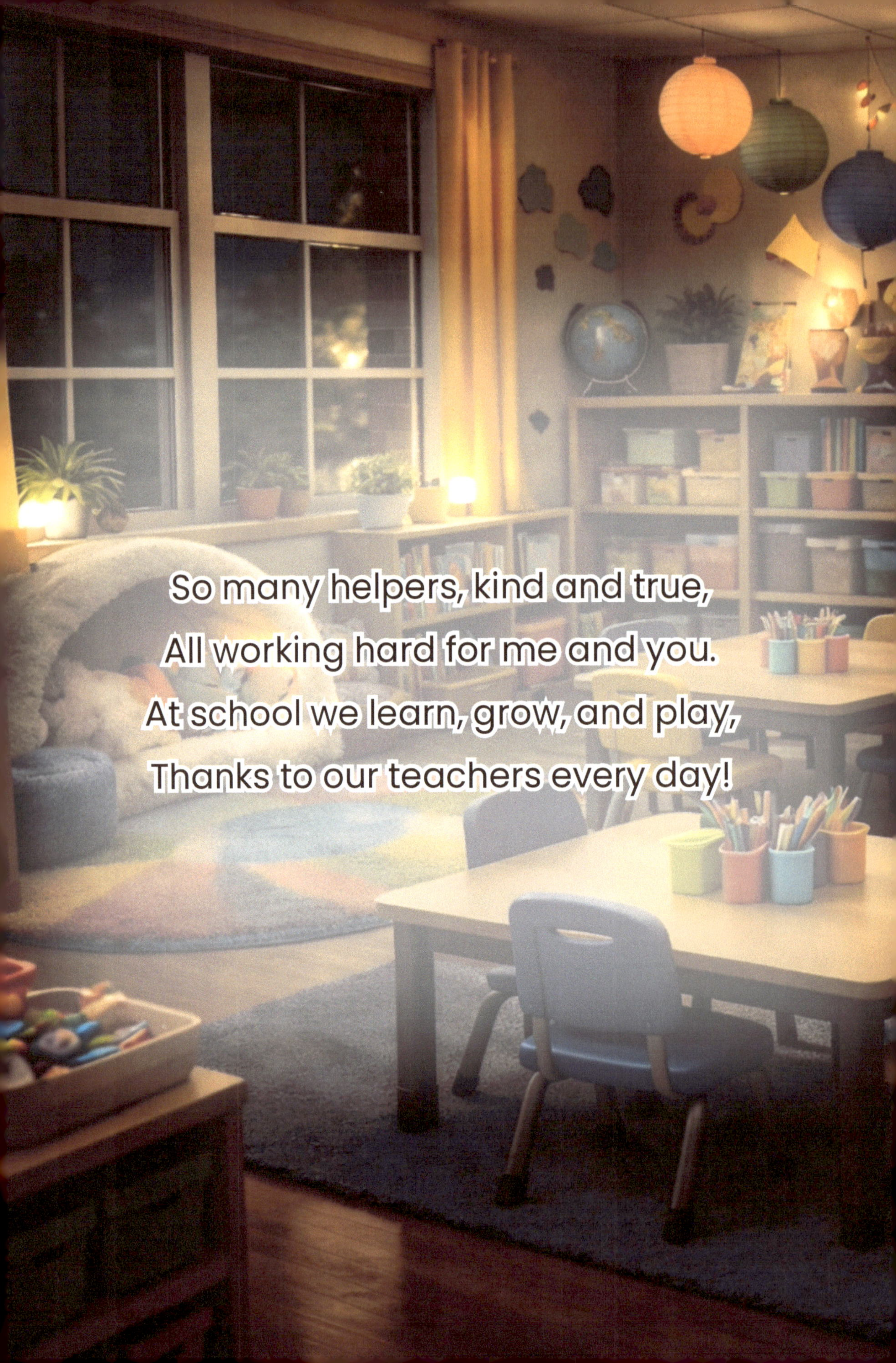

So many helpers, kind and true,
All working hard for me and you.
At school we learn, grow, and play,
Thanks to our teachers every day!

From My Heart to Yours

Write a note, memory, or wish for the person who will treasure this book.

Today's Date: ________________

DESIGN YOUR OWN Tapi

May this page find you again, years from now.

www.ingramcontent.com/pod-product-compliance
Lightning Source LLC
LaVergne TN
LVHW070158110826
845147LV00002B/441

* 9 7 8 1 9 7 2 0 7 1 2 3 6 *